I0620205

PLAY DUMB & SABOTAGE

Mindfully under-anticipating
the child's needs and creating
opportunities to practice language.

JEANEEN TANG, MS, CCC-SLP

Speech-Language Pathologist

Printed by selfpublishing.com in the United States of America

First printing 2024

selfpublishing.com
PO Box 26556
Greenville, SC

www.playdumbandsabotage.com

ISBN: 979-8-89109-902-9 - paperback
ISBN: 979-8-89109-903-6 - ebook
ISBN: 979-8-89109-904-3 - hardcover

This book was written for my fellow speech-language pathologists, our assistants, along with every educator, parent, and caregiver who have the pleasure of playing a role in the development of our youth. No one can do it alone.

To my son, Che, who is the bravest person I've ever known. I'm honored to be your mom.

TABLE OF CONTENTS

ACKNOWLEDGEMENTS

Although I learned a lot about speech-language therapy in graduate school, I really didn't grasp the application of the concepts with children until I started working with some amazing speech-language pathologists in the Department of Education in Honolulu, Hawaii. My clinical fellow supervisor, Kathy Maemori, was outstanding. I was her first clinical fellow, but I wouldn't be her last. She went on to mentor many clinical fellows, as well as graduate students at the University of Hawaii, Manoa, after she retired from the DOE.

There wasn't a day that went by that I didn't call her to ask her opinion, get strategies, or just to talk about a frustrating day. I was hungry and eager to hone my skills in order to be a good therapist. At first, having to work with a full caseload of students with varying degrees of speech-language needs was overwhelming. Working with the children was one thing, and working with their parents was a whole different story.

Fast forward to over twenty years later, I found myself mentoring other speech-language pathologists and speech-language pathology assistants. I learned through mentoring that I cherished the excitement of seeing someone else grasp a concept or strategy for the first time. I'd taken for granted the simple things and nuances I had been performing for so many years that have become second nature. Seeing someone learn and apply these simple things made me realize I wanted to be able to have a broader reach and greater influence.

I had the idea of writing a book for speech therapy strategies early on in my career. I put the idea of the book on the back burner because I didn't know where to start. After mentoring new speech language pathologists and speech language pathology assistants, along with countless parents, teachers, and other educators, I realized I needed to write this book.

I want to thank every speech-language pathologist and educator that I learned from, as well as every child I've had the opportunity to work with. Without these people, I would not be the therapist I am today. I am ready to share my knowledge with all of you.

I appreciate all of the families I've worked with over the years. I feel blessed to have taught so many children and educated so many parents through my many years working in the school system and early intervention population.

I have to give a big shout out to the amazing team at Mind Of The Noise for bringing to life my ideas through their illustrations within the book. Alexis and Jason Harris' background in working with children with special needs gave them a unique perspective when helping me piece together the visuals I needed to communicate the strategies clearly for my readers.

There's one more person I have to dedicate this book to. My son, Che, inspires me every day to be the best mom, person, and professional I can be. He is the bravest person I know. No one has a bigger heart. No one has better dance moves.

MY WHY

I get asked the question, "Do you do speech therapy with your son?" a lot, because my son is disabled, and I am a speech therapist. It makes sense that people would wonder that. What they don't realize is that I'm constantly doing speech therapy with him, but not in the discrete, tabletop way we envision speech therapy usually happening.

Here's a little background on my son, Che. He was born at full-term of thirty-nine weeks via Cesarean section. I had been in labor for forty hours and hoped to give birth naturally, but the hiccups of labor fated us otherwise.

His development was right on target. He started sitting up on his own around five and a half months, started crawling around nine months, and started toddling around twelve months. He babbled, he laughed, and he was perfectly normal—until he wasn't.

When they say life can change in an instant, they're absolutely correct. Just short of turning thirteen months old, Che was very curious, very strong, and very fast. Even though he still hadn't mastered walking, he could toddle. The night of his accident, he had toddled eleven steps—more than he'd ever done before.

I had just given him a bath, wrapped him up in a towel, placed him in the middle of our queen size bed, and remembered I forgot to grab the lotion. The bathroom was adjacent to the bedroom, so the lotion was just a few steps away. It was mere fractions of seconds really, but enough time for him to try to follow me. That's when he fell eighteen inches from the top of the mattress, past the box spring, and down to the wood laminate. It wasn't a far fall, but it was enough to give him a large subdural hematoma.

At first, we didn't realize he had gotten hurt so badly from such a short fall. He cried for thirty seconds to a minute, then went limp. We rushed him to the emergency room at Children's Hospital of Los Angeles. The CT scan revealed the large subdural hematoma, and before we could comprehend the magnitude of the situation, they were intubating him and rushing him off for an emergency craniotomy. A few days later, he had a massive stroke. Both injuries were on the left side of his brain.

Che lost fifty percent of his peripheral vision, had a feeding tube through his nose for a month, lived at the hospital for over two months, was intubated twice, and has right hemiparesis of the upper and lower extremities. Our perfectly normal child had become a child with significant special needs in a matter of an instant.

From the time he was born, I did speech therapy with my son. I can't help but use my strategies with all children, whether they are normal developing or have some kind of delay or disability. Since my son's injuries, I never stopped working with him every day on his speech and language. I may not explicitly sit him down to teach him, but with every interaction he and I have, I am mindfully shaping my behavior to help him become a more confident communicator.

Now that Che is eleven years old, it's the best feeling to be able to have conversations with him. He's so opinionated, and even argumentative at times. He's eleven going on fifteen. He is able to problem solve, recall details from conversations and movies, and is a great negotiator to get what he wants. Although he has made good progress over the years with language, he still needs to work on the subtle nuances of social language and pragmatics, which we'll continue to focus on as he enters adolescence. It's hard to imagine he'll be a teenager in just a few years.

I know Che has learned how to model language as well. From all the years of having language modeled for him, he's been able to demonstrate those same skills with younger children.

We were babysitting my friend Megan's young children. Her son was sixteen months old. He was starting to use some simple signs for "more" and "please," but had very limited verbal words. Che was great playing with the little boy, and I found him imitating the strategies I used with him when he was little. Che has watched me work with a number of young children over the years. It was amazing to watch him engage in language-based play with the little boy, simplify his speech, and attempt to have the boy imitate simple sounds and words.

Watching Che become a teacher of language made me realize how amazing the human brain can be. His stroke happened on the left side of his brain, which is typically where our language center happens. Based on his brain scan, you'd expect his language to be very poor, if anything at all. Through neuroplasticity, his brain was able to rewire itself, and create different pathways to access and store language function.

His love of music and dancing pairs synergistically with the words in the songs he sings, and the poetry of his conversations. He is a reminder that anything is possible, and everything can be made into something wonderful.

INTRODUCTION

It's hard to believe it's been over twenty years that I have been in the profession of speech-language pathology. Over the years, I've worked with every age group, from early intervention, to school age, to adults. I came to this profession by a sort of happenstance.

When I was in the second grade, I wanted to be a teacher. After my grandfather passed away when I was eight years old, I started to have the desire to help people. I saw how difficult it was for him to get around at the end of his life. I was so young then, and felt so helpless.

When I was getting ready for my undergraduate studies, I really thought I wanted to become a physical therapist. I wanted to be that person who could help people like my grandfather. I also loved language arts. I knew, in order to become a physical therapist, I'd have to go to graduate school. So, for my undergraduate degree I did something completely different. I majored in English literature, with a minor in Creative Writing. I made sure I took all of my science prerequisites.

When it came time to apply to physical therapy school, I was torn. I thought I really wanted to go to PT school, but I also loved language, and considered getting a master's in fine arts to become an English professor. That's when someone suggested becoming a speech therapist.

At the time, I didn't really have much exposure to speech therapy. My best friend's mother was a speech therapist, but

I'd never seen her at work. When I found out my hometown university, the University of Hawaii, Manoa, had a speech therapy program, I was convinced I should at least give it a shot, and I'm glad I did.

During the program, I had amazing professors who taught their specialties. Memorizing the facts of anatomy, physiology, phonetics, and language development was challenging. Then applying what we learned in textbooks into real clinical situations, was a whole other set of obstacles and learning curves.

Although I learned a lot during graduate school, I really owe it to my mentor and supervisor, Kathy Maemori, for making me the clinician I am today. I must have called her every day during the nine months she oversaw me as I completed my clinical fellowship. There were little fires to put out every day, and occasional big fires along the way too. By watching and learning from Kathy and some of my fellow speech therapists, I was able to hone my skills, stay calm, and survive my way through my first year and many more.

I remember telling my brother, Jayson, years ago how I wanted to write a book about behaviors and language development. He said that no one would trust me, because I wasn't a parent. At that point, I'd been working with children for three or four years. I thought he was crazy at first, but I could understand where he was coming from.

I worked with special education students in the public school system. I loved my job. It was really hard work, and I would go home mentally drained, but I loved it. I thought it was great to work with special needs children, but could never have fathomed at the time that I could ever have a special needs child of my own.

Then in 2012, I had my son, Che. He was great. He developed normally all the way until his thirteenth month of life. Then he had a tragic accident. He fell off the bed and suffered a subdural hematoma. He underwent an emergency craniotomy and a few days later he had a stroke. The long-term effects of his injuries included right hemiparesis, bilateral hemianopia, attention deficits, cognitive deficits, and most recently, seizure. My normal son was now a child with special needs.

Now, not only was I a mother, but also the mother to a child with special needs. I gained a greater perspective and level of empathy to those parents and caregivers I had interacted with, all the years prior to my son's injuries. I realized being a parent and a therapist enabled me to see two sides of the coin, and I could play devil's advocate in meetings to relate to the caregivers of my clients better.

I wanted to write this book to be a handbook for anyone who works or interacts with children, whether the child has special needs or not. The strategies are meant to be applicable to children across the board in many different environments, whether it be in the home, preschool, elementary school, or out in the community. I wanted this book to be more of a conversation, than a textbook. It's meant to be easily understood by everyone, from professionals to every day individuals. The lessons, strategies, and examples can be learned and passed on to a greater audience through you. I hope you find the content relatable, and also refreshing.

I hope by the end of this book, you have a better understanding of, and excitement for, language development and communication. My goal isn't for you to finish this book and then feel like you've mastered the complex development of speech and language, but instead to introduce it, and encourage you to practice with your own children.

If you feel like you are better equipped to help demonstrate and develop communication in your youngsters, give yourself a pat on the back. It's not easy to learn and apply some of these strategies. It may feel unnatural at first, but eventually, with consistent practice, it'll become a habit that you no longer have to think about.

It's been my pleasure to work with this young population for over two decades now. I've enjoyed teaching and coaching the parents, the teachers, and other educators and therapists of the many children that I've come across in my professional career. I wanted to be able to reach a broader audience, and make a bigger impact in the development of speech and language. Thank you for the opportunity to help make this dream come true.

I want to be accessible to everyone, although that seems like a lofty goal. Through this handbook, you will learn the strategies, and in turn be able to use them with your own children. Through you, I am able to stretch my ideas outward and beyond my imagination.

If you find yourself with any questions on the strategies, would like to attend one of my training sessions, or would like me to do a training with your organization, please feel free to reach out. I'd love to connect with you, as you are the gateway to the world.

Aloha,
Jeaneen Tang, MS, CCC-SLP

www.playdumbandsabotage.com

HELPFUL TERMS

- **Receptive Language** - The ability to understand and comprehend spoken language that you hear or read.
- **Expressive Language** - The ability to communicate our thoughts and feelings through words, gestures, signs, and/or symbols.
- **Apraxia of Speech** - A neurological disorder that affects the brain pathways involved in producing speech.
- **Expressive Aphasia** - A type of aphasia characterized by partial loss of the ability to produce language (spoken, manual, or written), although comprehension generally remains intact.
- **Target Item** - The particular word, vocabulary, or item the activity is focused and utilizing to develop language.
- **Carrier Phrase** - The words in the phrase are the same, except for the ending.

CHAPTER 1

You're a Good Parent (Caregiver, Therapist, etc.)

Over-Anticipation

As parents, we want to show that we know exactly what our child needs, wants, and even thinks. We want to be "good" parents. In doing so, we watch like a hawk, listen like an elephant, and learn to anticipate their every move, analyze their every cry, facial expression, and grunt. We have them on a schedule, so we know when they should eat, drink, poop, and sleep.

The reasons for doing this are varied. Perhaps it is because we had "good" parents, and we want to be just like them. Or maybe it is because we had inattentive parents, and we want to be the exact opposite of them. Whichever it is, we find ourselves in this predicament of having everything ready for any situation. We have food ready and served before the child realizes they are even hungry. We change diapers at the first indication of wetness or foul smell. We surround them with every toy imaginable to keep them entertained. We're "good" parents.

In being "good" parents and caregivers, we have met the child's needs and wants. We have proven to ourselves that we are "on top of things." Our friends commend us for being great parents, and we feel the satisfaction of having our child being content and provided for. But one must question if this honed skill of over-anticipation is truly helping the child develop, or if it is hindering the natural evolution of communication.

Sometimes it's easier to think for the child, instead of allowing them to grow into making choices for themselves. It's much easier for us to decide what clothes the child will wear, what they will eat for a snack or meal, and what toys they should have for the car ride. Just to imagine the time it would take to have them make their own choices, would make any parent or caregiver on a tight schedule anxious, and probably late for every appointment or planned errand.

However, if we're thinking for the child before the child needs to think for themself, we've taken away the introduction to, and key practice of, communication. Only with opportunities and repetition can the child develop the skills of understanding and expression. By over-anticipating, we are doing the child a disservice, even if we may have the best of intentions.

We're all guilty of over-anticipating for our children. Even I have planned and prepared without really taking into consideration my son's true desires and wants. Does he want to wear the blue shirt or green shirt? Who cares—we're late! He's wearing the blue shirt, and that's final. He's having a banana and milk for a snack. He's going to play with Elmo, and he's going to love it. I've been there, done that, and it's okay. It's how we move forward that counts.

Play Dumb: Mindful Under-anticipation

As much careful thought and planning as it takes to over anticipate a child's needs, it takes even more thought and planning to under-anticipate a child's needs. This is not to say that we should ignore the child and their needs. Instead, we should know what the child needs, then mindfully resist the habit to react before the need is communicated by the child. It takes more work to mindfully under-anticipate than it does to anticipate. This concept may be confusing at first, but it can be seen in examples of every-day practices.

As good caregivers, we are prepared. If it's snack time, we have the plate or bowl out. We've filled their dish with a bountiful amount of their favorite food, and their drink vessel with their yummiest beverage. You have napkins or burp cloths ready at hand for any wiping up of messes. Everything is ready and set. You get an "A" for effort.

You put in the effort, but how does your effort pay off for the child? They're happy with satisfied taste buds and tummies. The child is content. You are content. You were thoughtful. The child is clean. You're happy about that too. The child did not have to think at all. You probably never thought about that part, did you?

Toddlers and young children aren't ready to get their own snacks and things ready. If we tried to let them do that, they'd just make a big mess that we need to clean up anyways. But now, we are over-anticipating, and the child does not get a chance to start learning.

We can change this approach very easily. Let's say instead, you only place three cheese puffs in the bowl, and only fill the cup a quarter of the way. The child will still be hungry and thirsty after they have finished what was given. How could you leave the child hungry and thirsty? That's not good caregiving, or is it?

Caregiving is not only providing for the child, but also developing the child's mind, their physical being, and their communication. When you're good at preparing for the child, that's a reflection of your work. It's an instant outward proof of the effort you put in. When you help to develop the child's cognition, the product of your work with them might take a while to be evident because it takes time. However, with practice and repetition, you will help their ability to navigate their world, to understand others, and express themselves.

As caregivers, we know what every little grunt, whine, or any other vocalization is trying to communicate. We are right there with their favorite toy, favorite snack, or favorite drink. With just the littlest reach towards something, we are right there giving the item to the child, without hesitation.

This is heightened further once children are able to say words, as they get away with saying just, "juice," or "ball," and getting what they want. Depending on the level the child is functioning at, there are ways to offset this. I might respond with, "Juice, I love juice," or "Juice, yes, that's juice. Did you want something?" I am modeling the vocabulary for the child which I would like them to absorb, and then be able to express.

Oftentimes, it is best to start by modeling the full sentence for the child, even if they cannot immediately recreate it, such as, I want juice, please." The child may only be able to say, "juice, please," or "want juice." The key is to stretch their abilities just further than what they are able to demonstrate independently.

Some children are non-verbal, or have very little babbling and vocalizations. For these children, they may rely on the use of simple signs, and can get away with just trying to vocalize something similar to "juice." Sometimes a child's vocalizations sound nothing like the target sound or words, and that's okay. As long as the child is putting in the effort to experiment with communication, we can count that as their conversational turn.

Story of Kane

When my godson, Kane, was nine months old, he was a very dependent child. He would not budge an inch across the floor. He hadn't learned to crawl yet, or even slither his body to get from point to point . He was a big baby, but that was no excuse for him to just lie there. He would get picked up and carried, was fed on schedule, and had no need to really put in the work.

It wasn't until one day when he was over visiting, that he really started getting his body moving across the floor. It didn't happen all at once. It didn't really happen at all—at first. He did his usual lying down on his back, his arms and legs moving about but not taking him anywhere. Then, cue the rainbow slinky. His eyes widened, and his appendages flayed around in excitement. I brought the slinky close to him, but out of reach. He extended a hand for it, but I didn't just hand it over. I continued to shake it about near him, then draw it away. His excitement continued as his eyes locked in on the prize.

With one more tempting dangle, just out of reach, I then placed the slinky on the ground about a foot away from his fingertips. He started to complain, whine, and pout. His body didn't move towards the slinky, as he was used to having things done for him. Then, something changed. He wasn't getting his way, and no one was giving him the easy way out. He started to wriggle his body until he finally turned over.

This was a huge improvement for him. Now on his belly, he began to swim in place, his arms still unable to pull him along, and his legs not pushing hard enough. We could tell by his noises that he was reaching frustration. I waved off his mother, who desperately wanted to hand Kane the slinky. We knew what he wanted. He knew what he wanted. It was time for him to work for what he wanted.

Slowly, Kane started getting traction with his arms and legs. His spine moved his body in a side-to-side motion, with his arms and legs now in concert. His eyes were locked on the slinky. His movements continued to get bigger and more coordinated, until he finally moved forward, ever so slightly. He was doing it, and we cheered him on as he inched his way forward. He now was in control of his own body, and could maneuver through space to get what he desired. He finally reached out and grasped the slinky like he'd found buried treasure.

Let's Practice

Applying strategies to your real-life situations may seem difficult at first, but if you start with small steps, you can slowly build the strategies into habits that will benefit your child and other children you interact with.

Here are ways you can start incorporating "playing dumb" into your daily routine. You will need to adjust the level in which you play dumb with a child based on their level of communication. These examples are for children with adequate receptive language (the ability to understand or comprehend) and some expressive language (the ability to use speech to communicate). These are meant to make the child question the routines, so they can begin to learn for themselves. Fill in the last line with your own idea.

- ❖ Getting dressed:
    - Putting underwear or pants on your or the child's head.
    - Putting socks on your hands.
    - Pull out two shirts to put on.
    - Put on pants first, then underwear over the pants.
    - _____

- ❖ Grooming:
    - Give the child the toothpaste tube, but no toothbrush.
    - Pretend to brush your teeth with a hairbrush.
    - Pretend to brush your hair with your toothbrush.
    - _____

- ❖ Meals and Snacks
  - Serve cereal without milk.
  - Pretend like you are going to pour orange juice over cereal.
  - Give them a fork with soup
  - Place the plate or bowl on the table, but out of reach.
  - Give them a cup without anything in it.
  - Give a plate or bowl without anything in it.
  - _____

- ❖ School/Homework Time:
  - Provide paper, but no writing utensil.
  - Provide a writing utensil, but no paper.
  - _____

- ❖ Bedtime
  - Hold a book upside down.
  - Start reading from the back of the book.
  - Don't put the blanket on the child.
  - Cover them with a hand towel instead of a blanket.
  - Cover them with a pillow instead of a blanket.
  - Walk out of the room with their pillow.
  - _____

CHAPTER 2

No Child Has Ever Died of Crying (as far as we know)

Whose Kid is Crying?

We've all heard a child crying in a restaurant, on an airplane, or in a movie theater. Maybe that child was yours. Maybe you were on a date, and the crying was really ruining the mood. Either way, we've all had the thought, "Whose kid is crying?" That thought is usually accompanied with the urgent thought of, "Make that kid stop crying," or "What kind of parents does that child have?"

I've been there. My son has cried. I've heard other children cry. If you have children or are even near children, you're eventually going to hear crying. That is not at all a pleasant sound. Our initial instinct is to find a way to make the crying stop. If you are not the one caregiving for the child, you are praying that whoever is taking care of the child will make the crying stop. For the most part, everyone would like the crying to stop.

While it may be annoying, the real and deeper reason for wanting our child to stop crying, is based on our own embarrassment. We are uncomfortable with the attention it causes in public. People are looking at us, judging us, and maybe some are empathizing with us. Mostly, they're judging us—so we think. We're so quick to shush the crying, we become detached from the communication between the child and ourselves. We stop listening to the message behind it, and start trying to block everything out.

Trying to block out crying is really a useless tactic. The child is crying, they're not going anywhere, and if you try to block it out, chances are the noise is going to get louder, attract more negative attention, and you'll end up being even more uncomfortable. It's best practice to deal with the child and situation at hand. In the end, working through crying will make you a better listener, problem solver, and caregiver.

Crying is Communication

Before we can deal with a crying child, we must first understand why children typically cry. When they're babies, they mainly cry due to three basic needs: they're hungry, wet, or tired. They cry because they need to be fed, need to be changed, or need to rest. Crying is a baby's first way of communication. The first sound we hear from a baby is crying, and it is a welcomed cry, letting us know that the baby is alive, strong, and thriving.

We've all known of a baby that was "inconsolable," right? Maybe they were colicky, sick, or hurt. Maybe they really were inconsolable. Either way, it seemed as if nothing would be able to soothe the baby. You've tried rocking them, patting them, changing their diaper, singing several songs, or the intentional and prolonged, "Shhhhhhh. . ." When a baby doesn't stop crying, minutes can feel like hours, and your head can feel like earthquake tremors.

As babies get a little older, the basic crying evolves into the next step in communication. Babies quickly learn that they can get the attention of adults through crying. Babies may not always know what exactly they are trying to communicate, but they are aware that they create some kind of reaction in the people surrounding them.

Pay attention to me!
Yes! Look at me!
Hey, I'm awake now!
Get me out of this crib.
I want to be carried.
I want to be put down.
I'm hot.
I'm cold.
I want a hug!!!

Children learn to cry to communicate they're upset, frustrated, and sometimes because they don't want to do the work. Sometimes it can be embarrassing, upsetting, or downright frustrating for the caregiver, and anyone within earshot of the crying child. Our initial reaction to a child crying in public is to shush them frantically, in order to not out yourself as the caregiver of the unruly child. It takes practice and mindful action to remain calm in the face of chaos. It's similar to meditation through pain, I'd imagine.

In situations when our child is crying, remember to take a breath, ground yourself, and connect with the child. Assess what could be the cause of the crying. Run through this checklist:

- Are they hurt?
- Are they wet/dirty?
- Are they hungry?
- Are they tired?
- Are they hot?
- Are they cold?
- Are they looking at something they "want"?
- Are they reaching for something they "want"?

If you've run through the checklist and still haven't been able to quiet the chaos, don't give up. Pull out all the goofy tricks you can think of. Act like a silly animal, or dangle fun toys to engage them. Maybe they want to be held. Maybe they want nothing to do with you. Whatever it is, there is likely a solution. It might just be more difficult to solve than you'd like.

The Fine Line Between Stretching Abilities and Inability

There is a fine line between a child's ability and inability to do a task. You would never ask a child who was crawling to climb a set of stairs, but you may ask a child who was toddling to walk a few more steps to their target. You would not ask a child who is barely babbling to imitate a sentence, but you may ask that same child to closely approximate a single word or syllable, in order to request a desired item.

It's very important to be able to observe, assess, and adjust when working with a child. First, you must be able to take in the whole picture to observe their ability to understand and express. Then, you can assess to see what they are able to communicate, and what directions they can follow. From there, you can adjust your interactions to meet the child at where they can be successful.

If a child is functionally non-verbal, with minimal to no vocalizations and sounds, you may have them try to imitate a sign for "more" or "please" to request a desired item. They may require hand-over-hand assistance in order to perform the simple signs. The most ideal way of introducing simple signs is to have a communicator in front of the child, holding the desired item, and a silent prompter in the back of the child to provide the hand-over-hand modeling from behind the child. When you prompt a child from the front as the communicator, the child may become reliant on your prompting and wait for your model before performing the sign. By having the silent prompter, prompt from behind, you take away some of the visual prompting, and eventually fade away the physical prompts as the child builds the skill, and is successful in spontaneously utilizing the sign with the communicator.

Having a silent prompter from behind the child is ideal, but if that is not available, you can make it work. You may need to do hand-over-hand modeling for the child from in front of the child to grasp the concept of doing a sign in order to get a desired item. The sign should be accompanied by the vocabulary you are trying to introduce, such as "more," or "please." You can start to pull back on the physical prompts, and demonstrate only the visual model of the sign. Then, once the child is able to consistently imitate the modeled sign, you can pull back even further, and only provide the verbal cues. Once the child is able to demonstrate the appropriate sign with the verbal cue provided, you can pull back again, and not provide a verbal or physical prompt, instead just presenting the desired item in view, but out of reach.

You may introduce imitating the initial sounds of the target item, such as "bah" for "ball." The first sound of a word is the bookend to a morsel. If you can say the first sound, you can link together the additional sounds to form the whole word. Each sound of a word can be imagined as a car of a train, one after another until the whole train is complete.

Once the child is able to consistently babble with various sounds and intonation, you may graduate them to imitating single target words, such as, "ball," or, "bubble." The production may be a close, or gross, approximation of the word, and that is okay. The imitation of the intonation which you model the word should be similar.

Once a child demonstrates the ability to do a task or skill, you can then hold out on the reward until the task or skill is completed to the fullest. For instance, if a child has been able to say a full sentence to request for items or activities, such as, "I want the ball, please," and they are only telling you, "ball," you can hold out on giving the child the ball.

Withholding a desired item will seem unnatural at first. Purposely allowing a child to whine or cry will feel uncomfortable, but if done correctly and consistently, you'll find the child will learn to use their words more readily and independently. It's not beneficial for the child if you do a great job withholding a desired item one time, and then give in the next time they pull at your heart strings. The key point to remember is that you are stretching them to grow when you present opportunities to utilize new language, and you are only inhibiting their growth when you enable them to get what they want without doing the work.

The Story of Everly

When I first started working with Everly, she was three years old. She was able to say a lot of words, but she often babbled in jargon people weren't able to understand. She would get frustrated when she didn't get what she wanted, and would throw huge tantrums on the ground. She would cry and yell, roll around on the ground, and sometimes kick. Her teachers would try to keep her safe and away from her peers, so no one would get hurt. Everly's tantrums were a daily occurrence, if not multiple times a day.

The director of her preschool met with Everly's parents, and it was agreed that she would benefit from speech therapy to help with her communication, and hopefully with her behaviors. Her parents choose to go the private route for speech therapy, rather than through special education, because Everly was intelligent, just not intelligible.

I soon found out she knew a lot of shapes, colors, and names to many things. She was able to name things she wanted to play with, but was not able to ask for things appropriately with a question. She was quite demanding in her requests, such as, "Give me it," or "That's mine."

For Everly, her crying and tantrums stemmed from her gap between what she wanted to communicate, and her inability to verbally express herself correctly. She really wanted to be understood, and to get her message across to peers and staff. Although she had a number of words in her vocabulary, stringing them together in an organized manner was difficult. I found that if she didn't have the words for a concept or item, she produced more jargon and unintelligible speech. When she wasn't understood, that's when she would pout, cry, yell, and throw herself down to the ground.

Today, Everly is four years old and is able to communicate her needs, wants, and ideas using three to four-word utterances. She is able to imitate longer utterances, to increase the detail and specificity of her communication. Although she will occasionally still have tantrums, they are no longer due to her inability to communicate, but rather her independent personality.

Let's Practice

What are three things your child would "die" for? Is it a food? Is it a toy? Is it an activity such as bubbles or a light show? Write them here.

1. _____

2. _____

3. _____

Here are some ideas to encourage communication with food:

- Portion out the food into small amounts, such as five goldfish crackers, a quarter of a cookie, or two grapes.
- Use a container for food that the child can't open without assistance.
- Put the food in sight, but out of reach.

Here are some ideas to encourage communication with toys:

- Put the toy on a shelf or high place where the child can see it, but not reach it. Make sure the child doesn't try to climb up to get it.
- Play with the toy yourself to tempt the child to want to play with the toy more.

Here are some ideas to encourage engagement with activities:

- Set a timer.
- Utilize a token board to make it into a game or a way to earn a prize.
- Do the activity yourself, and make it seem really fun.

CHAPTER 3

Don't Ask Yes or No Questions (unless you're willing to honor the no)

Biggest Take Away

One of the first, and most important, lessons I learned as a new speech-language pathologist was to stop asking yes or no questions. . . unless you are willing to honor the no. It's a lesson that I've continued to pass along to my fellow educators, parents of clients, and anyone else who happens to interact with a child. It's a really important lesson, and here's why.

If you ask a child, "Are you ready to work?" and they reply, "no," what do you do then? Do you encourage them to work? Bribe them to work? Tell them they're going to work anyways? No. You must honor the "no." You asked a question, and you got an answer.

A common one we find ourselves asking is, "Can you say ___?" If they answer, "no," that's the end of that one. When I teach this concept to parents, therapists, and other caregivers, a lightbulb goes on. They usually haven't been introduced to this notion of the need to honor the no, if a closed question is asked.

As parents, we've all asked the most important question at snack/mealtime, "Do you want ____?" We've all gotten the answer, "no," at some point. We then continue to investigate by following up with, "Do you want (different thing)?" We get another, "no." This series of yes or no questions can get you running in circles, and you may never find out what the child wants.

Stay Away from These Questions

We've all been guilty of asking a Y/N question, getting a "no" answer, then trying to convince the child that they didn't really mean "no," and they can still do the task we wanted them to do. I've been there. Every parent I've worked with has been there. So has every therapist, teacher, and caregiver whom I've come across. It's okay, it happened. Acknowledge it, promise yourself you'll do better, and move on.

Some of the common question errors include:

- *Can you* say ____?
- *Can you* (do) ____?
- *Can you* put the ball in the bucket?
- *Are you* ready to work?
- *Do you want* to do ____?
- *Would you like* to play with ____?
- *Can you* show me the ____?
- *Do you want* to try this one?
- *Do you want* to clean up?

How to Phrase the Question

I find the way you phrase questions needs to be done in a very methodical and mindful way. Without first thinking, our brains often automatically ask Y/N questions. It took a lot of practice to be able to eliminate them from my dialogue. Still to this day, I sometimes need to remind myself to be wary of slipping into simple Y/N questions that may get me a "no" answer, and lead me nowhere but back to square one.

To avoid these questions, you must provide options. Keep it simple, like "Would you like A or B?" When you provide options rather than ask Y/N questions, you are inferring two things are available to have or do, and the child gets to choose which one will be done. It also implies that an activity or item will be done no matter what.

Examples of questions:

- Would you like to eat an apple or banana?
- Which one would you like to do first, the car puzzle, or the numbers game?
- Would you like to do the shape puzzle, or read the book?

Use a Statement

The best way to get someone to do something is by telling them to do the task, rather than asking them if they can do the task. By being the director of their actions, you are able to strategically motivate them to do the target task. Although you may still be met with some defiance, this strategy works well more times than not.

When the goal is to get a child to repeat a target sound, word, or sentence, I never ask them to repeat it. I direct them to do it, but not in some pushy, demanding way. Trying to force a child (or anyone for that matter) to do or say anything, will get you nowhere but frustrated.

Examples of how you can phrase your direction to imitate include:

- "Your turn. You say it."
- "(Child's name), say ___."
- "Now, you try it. Say ___."

When the goal is to point to a target picture or item, you can also direct them, rather than ask them, to do so. Sometimes the child needs a model in order to understand what is being asked of them in the task. You may start with, "I see a dog. There's the dog (touch the dog). I see a cat. Show me the cat."

For children functioning at a low level, they may need hand-over-hand assistance to point to or touch a target item or picture. You would still give the same direction, "Touch the cat," but you would also assist in the movement of the child's hand and pointer finger to touch the cat.

Eventually, the goal is for you to be able to fade away the tactile prompting, and have the child be independent in completing the task. The way to fade away the tactile prompting is to allow for a pause between your verbal direction and engaging in tactile prompt. You may say, "Point to the car." Then you would wait for three to five seconds to assess whether or not the child is going to initiate the physical movement to do the task. If they haven't given you the slightest clue that they've processed the direction, and are ready to try it out, go ahead and point to the desired item or picture to model the direction. If the child still isn't able to copy what you did, then you can initiate the hand-over-hand assist to complete the task.

Let's Practice

What are some Y/N questions you find yourself asking on a daily basis? Here are a few examples:

- Are you ready to go?
- Can you get some socks?
- Can you clean up your toys?

Now, list the Y/N questions you've found yourself asking:

1. _____
2. _____
3. _____
4. _____
5. _____

Now, change each of them into five directive sentences:

1. _____
2. _____
3. _____
4. _____
5. _____

Your bonus assignment is to try avoiding using the following question starters for one day (then one more day at a time until it becomes a habit):

- Can
- Are

CHAPTER 4

Slow It Down

Understand what?

Have you ever learned a new language? Maybe you've traveled to another country and were immersed in a language you weren't familiar with. I'm currently trying to learn Spanish. I've been in Los Angeles for seventeen years now, and I thought it was about time I picked it up. Before I knew any Spanish, hearing the language sounded like white noise. I didn't understand any of it, and nothing sounded vaguely familiar. I didn't pay attention to what was being said, because it wasn't important or meaningful to me.

Now that I've completed several lessons, learned several keywords, and have even been able to form simple sentences and questions, when I hear people speaking Spanish, I automatically try to tune my ears in, and figure out what is being said. Unfortunately, I still struggle to understand Spanish spoken by native speakers in normal conversation. They speak too quickly for my ears and brain to decipher what is being said. Thankfully, most people are very forgiving, and attempt to understand my entry level Spanish skills.

This is very similar to how we interact with children. When we speak at full speed, the child who struggles to express is likely also struggling to comprehend. It's like learning a new language. Even if they are being instructed in their primary language, it can be overwhelming for the child who has a language impairment.

It is our job as caregivers, who have a mastery of language, to assist children in language development. We are all somewhat educators, whether we have a degree in education or not. Parents are a child's first teachers. They learn from our modeling, our interactions, and our reactions.

We can do a simple thing to help the child understand and express better: slow down our speech. Slowing down our speech-modeling just a tiny bit, allows the child to process the sounds they hear, observe the motions of your mouth, and receive the facial expressions that go along with the whole message. Speech has a rhythm and cadence to it. The intonation, prosody, and pacing, shape how language is translated and understood.

Tap it Out, Clap it Out

We have five senses, and should utilize as many of them as possible to reinforce learning. We can't taste or smell syllables, but we can sure hear them. We can also visualize and feel them. Using a multimodal sensory approach to introducing language, is a great way to solidify understanding, and promote learning.

If you've ever played a musical instrument or studied singing, you may have had to learn how to read musical notes. The type of note tells you the length of the sound being played, the beat of the music, and the tone or pitch at which the note is played or sung. Musical notes written on paper is one way of seeing sound and understanding how the sounds should be played out. It would be great if we could relay the sounds and syllables for words in the same manner, but not everyone understands how to read sheet music.

When you clap or tap our syllables, our eyes see our hands or feet move. We get visual input from watching our bodies. We can also utilize external factors to help with visualizing sounds and syllables. You can use anything from colored dots, a line of cars, a sequence of building blocks, or even lights to signify the sounds of the syllables, and the beat at which the words are produced. Words have a rhythm all their own. Some words are spoken faster than others. Some syllables are given more emphasis than others. The sounds and syllables in words are meant to be varied, just like the music we listen to. Monotony doesn't have a place in human speech, so we should not model monotone speech.

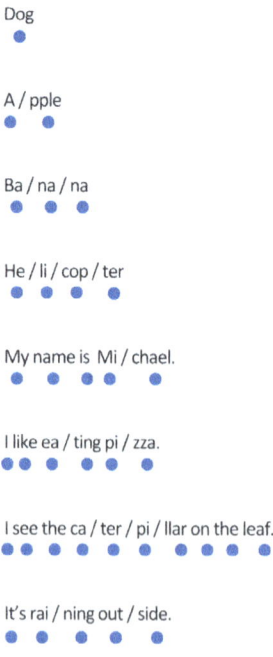

Clapping Out and Tapping Out Practice

How many syllables are in the following sentences?

1. My name is Michael.
2. I like to eat ice cream.
3. I see an elephant.
4. I want to eat a strawberry.
5. The elephant and the giraffe live in the safari.

Now, clap or tap out the syllables as you say each sentence aloud to yourself. Once you've mastered clapping out or tapping out the syllables of the sentences, you can then practice having the child clap or tap out each of the sentences with you.

Talk Touch Activities

Another way of slowing down a child's speech is to utilize a system to pace out the individual words of a sentence. Children may sometimes say a sentence very quickly, making the words jumble together and the sentence unintelligible.

I like to put out blocks or simply draw out familiar shapes such as squares, circles, or stars, that the child can touch when imitating sentences. The idea is that the child will be able to slow down their speech production of the sentence by having to pace out each individual word.

You will model the activity for the child by saying the sentence and touching in individual shape or item for each word in the sentence. You should be demonstrating a slower pace than your normal speech. If the child is unable to copy you on their own, you may need to first guide their hand and help them point the shapes or items. The next step toward independence is having the child point to the shape or item at the same time you do. Once they are able to mirror you, you can decrease your assistance more and more until they progress to performing the task completely on their own.

The   frog   jumps   very   high.

Sing-Songy

Have you ever noticed how you can remember the words to a song you haven't heard in years, but you can't for the life of you remember the words of the presentation you spent all night preparing? Just hearing a familiar tune or melody brings back the words that paired with it. This is because The right and left hemispheres of our brain have different jobs. Most people have their language center in the left hemisphere. Our left hemisphere typically is responsible for language and logic. There is organization and order in understanding and expressing language, and in producing speech.

Most people access creativity from the right hemisphere of their brain. Although the art of music is thought to be creativity, there is also a logic to music, such as the rhythm and order of musical notes. We can think of creativity as being chaotic at times, but there are also boundaries set in order to make sense of the chaos.

When we incorporate both hemispheres of the brain, we are able to strengthen the learning and recall of information. Integration of both sides of the brain increases communication across hemispheres and neurons. Music with words accesses both the right and left hemispheres of the brain.

An example of rehabilitation utilizing song is with apraxia of speech and expressive aphasia. Both deficits present as a lack of fluency in language. By integrating music, rhythm, and language, we can often get fluency in speech in a song or musical version of a sentence, where purely spoken speech would be halted or completely absent.

A child is likely to start humming or singing a nursery rhyme before they are able to say simple sentences, even though the string of words in a song may be longer than a short sentence of three to four words. The combination of the melody, repetition of words, and sometimes accompanying movements, such as in "The Itsy-Bitsy Spider," "Twinkle, Twinkle, Little Star," and "The Wheels on the Bus," work in concert to create auditory and sense memory, that will exist within the child for the rest of their lives.

I often incorporate the melody of a common nursery rhyme and substitute the target utterances for the original lines. The melody is usually familiar, such as "Are You Sleeping? (Brother John)," which is typically paired with a common circle time song about what day of the week it is. "Today is Tuesday, today is Tuesday, all day long, all day long. . ." You can make up any lyrics to a melody of a nursery rhyme that suits your activity or topic of focus.

Here are a few examples of functional lyrics you can create following the same melody as "Are You Sleeping?"

I Like Pizza
> I like pizza.
> I like pizza.
> Yes, I do.
> Yes, I do.
>
> I like pizza
> I like pizza.
> How 'bout you?
> How 'bout you?

What Do We See?
> We see a red bird.
> We see a blue horse.
> What do you see?
> What do you see?
>
> We see a yellow duck.
> We see a green frog.
> That's what we see.
> That's what we see.

Sing It Out Practice

Think of a familiar and simple tune, like a nursery rhyme ingrained in your childhood memory. Here are a few I use quite often. Fill in the last line with something meaningful to you.

- Twinkle, Twinkle Little Star
- The Wheels on the Bus
- Where is Thumbkin?
- _____.

Now, let's add some of our own words to the melody, and see how it stays in our memory easier than if we just tried to recite it as a sentence. Let's try it with "Twinkle, Twinkle Little Star."

I want ice cream, yes, I do. (Twinkle, twinkle little star)
I want ice cream. How about you? (How I wonder what you are.)

What are some of your own words you can put to your favorite melody?

Elongate the Sounds

Within a word, all sounds are not created equally. Individually, you could say yes, but within a word, sounds may vary in their length and volume. If every sound was equal in length and volume, we would sound monotone. For children who are struggling in producing sounds and language, this could put them at risk of running all the sounds together and muddle their words.

Over the years, I've discovered that vowels are the nucleus of the words, while consonants act like bookends. Subconsciously, if you focus on producing a strong vowel sound, the consonants on either side of the vowels are also strengthened and articulated more distinctly..

Similarly, not all syllables are created equal. In a multisyllabic word, there will always be a strong syllable and a weak syllable. The stronger syllable will inevitably be the one where you'd stress elongation more. The elongated sound will more than likely be the vowel sound, rather than the consonant. Vowel sounds are able to be stretched in length and varied in volume more easily than consonants.

It's important to understand the segments of words and be able to model how to elongate the words so children can hear the variation in your voice and copy it in their own speech. So much of what we communicate is in the ebbs and flows of our tone, pitch, and volume.

Examples of elongating multisyllabic words include:

- Balloon: Bah – **loo**n
- Apple: **A** – puhl
- Bathroom: B**ath** – room
- Elephant: **E**h – luh- fant
- Tiger: T**ie** - ger

Emphasis is Important

What's the important part of the sentence? What are we supposed to pay attention to? How are we to distinguish what is a filler word, and what holds weight? We speak without really having to think about what exactly we are saying. Typically we think in real time, as we are saying something. We speak with a need to communicate an idea or message, and with the practice we've had for many years, and the words are formed without thinking about what we need to emphasize.

Emphasizing a word, or even a syllable of a word, helps it stand out from the other words and sounds. There are various ways you can emphasize a word, including varying the pitch or tone of the sounds, elongating the sounds, slowing down the speed of production, making the sound louder, or being extra animated.

Do you want to eat an *apple,* or do you want to eat a *banana?*

You may not think of emphasizing a pause in your speech, but it is one effective way in separating out the chaos into manageable pieces. When we write, we can see where there is a period, comma, or question mark. When we speak, we may not have the same awareness of where the unmarked punctuation is, but they are there, and they are valuable.

By adding a pause when we speak, we create anticipation and grab the listener's attention. What comes before the pause and what follows the pause is given greater meaning because the message has been presented in smaller chunks of information.

For example, when you tell someone your phone number or social security number, you will automatically group the numbers into socially agreed upon chunks rather than say the numbers in one continuous string. You wouldn't say, "5557416590." You'd say, "555-741-6590." By chunking the numbers together, the listener is able to grasp the smaller number sequences much easier and remember them more readily.

Whole Body Talking

Only a small portion of what we communicate is conveyed through words. We use several other forms of communication to get our messages across, including facial expressions, gestures, and intonation. There so much communicated outside of the letters and individual sounds of words that we don't even think about. Can you imagine sitting still and just saying words without using your hands, raising your eyebrows, varying your pitch, or producing a rising tone at the end of a question? It would sound similar to a robot with a monotone voice output system.

In our every day life, we are constantly utilizing gestures and body movements when we're talking with other people. If we want to relay a sense of excitement, our gestures are big, and our body movements may be extra dynamic. When we want to convey a sense of quiet and secrecy, we may make our bodies small, and move in the tiniest dimensions to reflect the tone of the message and situation.

The same applies to our voice. Our voice can vary in volume, pitch or tone, and rate or speed. If I'm talking to you from across the room, I'd need to use a loud volume, exaggerated movement of my articulators, a decreased rate so you can understand me, and probably a wide range of intonation in order to communicate my message clearly. If we're trying to talk in a movie theater while the trailers are playing, I'd have to use a very soft volume, breathy voice, a slow rate, and a more monotone pitch, so you can understand what I was saying.

It's important to model whole body talking for children because it helps them understand different emotions, the situation and context of conversations, and how they are able to imitate the same types of whole body talking when they practice interactions with other people. It can be helpful, and fun, to over exaggerate your whole body talking by imagining you are in a musical theater performance and you're trying to get the people in the back row to really see and hear you. Children will tend to mirror how they are spoken to and interacted with. By equipping them with a variety of communication tools, they will in turn become more effective communicators.

CHAPTER 5

That's Absurd!

Children absolutely love to be smarter than you. I haven't met one child who doesn't jump at the chance to tell me I'm wrong, or give me a stare to let me know I'm definitely wrong about something. It helps to build a child's confidence in communication by promoting a natural back and forth interaction between the child and the adult.

I was working with a little girl on verbs. We were looking at picture cards with various people demonstrating a number of different verbs. The little girl was able to name some of the verbs independently. I wanted her to start using longer utterances to form sentences to describe the verbs in the pictures.

I held up a picture of a woman smelling a flower. I asked the little girl, "What is she doing?" The little girl replied, "Smelling." That was great! She correctly labeled the target verb. But I wanted more.

I asked the little girl, "What is she smelling?" She didn't say anything. Hmmm. I asked her, "Is she smelling a dog?" She laughed and said, "No!" Hmmm. I asked her, "Is she smelling pizza?" She even louder and said, "No!" Hmmm. I asked her, "Then what is she smelling? She's smelling a . . ." And then she filled in the blank with, "flower."

Once they fill in the blank, you can work on stringing the words together to make a simple phrase or short sentence. Longer sentences can be delivered in bite sized, manageable chunks of one to two words a time. Once they can imitate two words at a time, move onto three, then four, and so on.

If the target sentence is, "She is smelling a white flower," you might break down the imitative task into smaller chunks as noted below. Each slash represents where you would break up the sentence into manageable segments. You would increase the number of words the child imitates at a time.

"Smelling flower"
"She is / smelling / a flower."
"She is smelling / a white flower."
"She is smelling a / white flower."
"She is smelling a white / flower."
"She is smelling a white flower.

Delivering longer sentences in smaller utterances helps the child build skills for teaching themselves other sentences they do not know. Moving forward, they can use this skill to master longer sentences independently.

Does a Dog Roar?

Animals and animal sounds are some of the very first things children learn. Children often make the sound of an animal before they are able to produce the name of it correctly. Association of animals to the sounds the animals make, helps to build comprehension. When the child is then able to produce the sound for the appropriate animal, they have demonstrated verbal expression.

Some ways to incorporate this into learning is to ask a series of questions and adding some absurd questions to get the child's attention, make the activity fun, and make them think they're smarter than you, such as:

- What does a sheep say?
- Does the sheep say, "Meow"?
- Does the sheep say, "Woof woof"?
- What does a sheep say? The sheep says. . . (Ideally, this is where the child will insert "Baa."). If they don't fill in the "baa," you can ask, "Does the sheep say 'meow'?" If they're familiar with animal sounds, they might tell you, "No!"

Here are some other fun absurd questions you can ask in different categories:

Clothing:
- Do we wear pants on our heads?
- Do you wear a jacket when you're hot?
- Do socks keep your ears warm?

Vehicles:
- Does a boat drive on the road?
- Does a car fly?
- Does an airplane go, "Vroom, vroom"?

Food:
- Are bananas blue?
- Should we put ketchup on ice cream?
- Is pizza sweet like cake?

Let's Practice

Think of some absurd questions you could ask about the following topics. Try to think of at least three.

FOOD

1. _____
2. _____
3. _____
4. _____
5. _____

ANIMALS

1. _____
2. _____
3. _____
4. _____
5. _____

CLOTHING

1. _____

2. _____

3. _____

4. _____

5. _____

BODY PARTS

1. _____

2. _____

3. _____

4. _____

5. _____

By incorporating absurd questions into your interactions and teaching, the activity is kept novel and dynamic, making the child more engaged and focused on the task. It's always helpful to make your activities fun and new for the child in order for active learning to happen.

I Really Like How the Fish Gallops

To work on their listening comprehension and attention skills, I like to introduce absurd statements into activities. When we hear statements that have conflicting information based on our understanding of the world, it's jarring, and causes our minds to question. Granted the child understands the concepts and characteristics of the target vocabulary, they should demonstrate a physical, and hopefully verbal, reaction to your absurd statement. That is, if they are listening to you.

Working on familiar categories and traits of the individual items within categories is a great way to hone your skills of making absurd statements. Categories such as clothing, animals, vehicles, and foods are some of the best places to start. Children have likely been exposed to items within each of these categories many times within their first few years of life. It's okay if their level of verbal expression is limited. They only have to comprehend what you are saying in order to benefit from the activity.

Let's take the category of clothing. What are the various traits or descriptors we use when talking about clothing, besides color and types of material?

- We wear clothes.
- We wear different pieces of clothing on different parts of our bodies.
- We wear different pieces of clothing during different seasons and temperatures of the year.
- Clothing is typically soft, not hard.
- We put clothing in drawers and closets.
- We hang some clothing on hangers.

- We wash clothes in a washing machine.
- We dry clothes in a dryer, or out in the sun.

Great! Now that we've listed a number of traits and descriptors for clothing, let's think of some absurd statements we could use for each one.

- I'm going to *eat* my shorts.
- You put socks on your *ears*.
- I should wear my tank top in the *snow*.
- My T-shirt is *hard*.
- Put the clothes in the *refrigerator*.
- Hang the shirt on an *umbrella*.
- Wash the clothes in the *toilet*.
- Dry the clothes in the *trash can*.

Let's Practice

Think of some absurd statements you could say about the following topics. Try to think of at least three.

FOOD

1. _____
2. _____
3. _____
4. _____
5. _____

ANIMALS

1. _____
2. _____
3. _____
4. _____
5. _____

CLOTHING

1. _____
2. _____
3. _____
4. _____
5. _____

BODY PARTS

1. _____
2. _____
3. _____
4. _____
5. _____

By interjecting absurd statements into your activities, you are able to keep the child's attention because they are listening for the next silly thing you might say. In turn, when the child is asked to make up an absurd statement, it causes them to use their imagination and creativity in a way they normally don't. Sometimes I find myself in a back and forth competition with a child to see who can think of the most absurd statement. We usually end up laughing so hard it hurts.

CHAPTER 6

Set Expectations

Kids Crave Structure

Children can be chaotic, loud, overactive, needy, messy, and kind of gross. Even the most active children crave structure. They don't even know they need it. They may fight tooth and nail against the idea of "being controlled," but in actuality, we all have a basic need of knowing what to expect.

Expectations can be thought of as mini jobs or goals we need to achieve, in order to gain something tangible, such as a toy, or intangible, such as praise or a compliment. We rarely do something for nothing. Even if we look at the simplest activity or chore of our own daily lives, we can see what the return or reward is.

We brush our teeth so we don't get cavities. We also brush our teeth so that we are socially accepted, and don't blow people away with foul breath. We sweep up the crumbs from the floor so we don't attract ants. We also sweep up the crumbs so we don't get yelled at by our housemates, and so we will possibly get thanked for doing so. We show up to work on time because that's when the workday starts. We also show up on time, in order to justify getting paid our full pay, as well as to support us in asking for a raise.

Children also require structure, in order to compartmentalize the chaos around them. My son and I devised a sorting system to put away toys, so he knows what toys belong where. Now, he can clean up his room independently with a few reminders to "keep going."Knowing where things "live" is helpful in organizing their minds as well as their environment. Children can learn that their clean clothes are found in their dresser drawer or closet, and their dirty clothes belong in the hamper. Teach them where they put their shoes, where they can find their toothbrush, where to find their favorite snacks, etc. Once they know where things are found, they know where to retrieve them from and where to return them to.

If we establish organization and structure at home, their initial environment, it'll be easier for them to translate that skill into other areas of life, such as at school or eventually work. If we don't demonstrate that skill ourselves, don't fret. You can still learn to become organized as an adult. It takes consistency to build a good habit, but that persistence will ultimately benefit yourself and your children tremendously. So, it's never too late to start.

Visual Schedules

Do you have a planner? I do. I have a paper planner, which a lot of people think is archaic, but I love it. I tried using only my digital calendar on my smartphone, but found myself frustrated scrolling through dates to figure out my schedule. I enjoy turning my pages and seeing everything laid out in front of me. I color code events, add cool stickers, and even draw fun designs to make things stand out.

Without my planner, I'd be lost. I probably couldn't recall my schedule for today, let alone what I did last Tuesday or even yesterday. Sometimes I think it's pretty sad that I rely on an external thing to assist with my ever-foggy (parent) memory, but I do, and it's a strategy that works for me.

What about our kiddos? What works for them? Who is keeping track of their day-to-day schedules? Probably not them. It's Mom and Dad, their teachers, their nannies, or even their therapists. This can cause our little guys to go through their day being told what to do, not knowing what to expect next, which means that they are in a constant state of uncertainty. What if this was how your day went, every day? Would it create a sense of anxiety, apprehension, worry, or even stubbornness? It could. Maybe, maybe not, but I'd lean on the side of yes.

I've found that when children know what to expect, they perform better overall. They are no longer in a state of unknowing. They have something for them to refer to, which anchors them to what is happening in the present. Referencing of a schedule can be done in various ways, such as auditorily, visually, or both combined. I have found that a purely auditory method of reference requires a higher level of skill, so starting with a combined auditory and visual strategy works best for introducing a schedule, especially for little children.

A visual schedule is a tool we can utilize, not only in the therapy room, but at home, in the classroom, and even mobily by having a portable one you could travel with in the car. A visual schedule is individual to each child, just like your planner is to you.

A visual schedule could consist of pictures, words, or a combination of the two.. For treatment sessions, I like to keep the number of items on the schedule to no more than five or six. If the child is very young, it might be best to start with only two to four items on a schedule, and then graduate to a more mature list of items as they become accustomed to the use of the schedule.

Ideas for schedules:

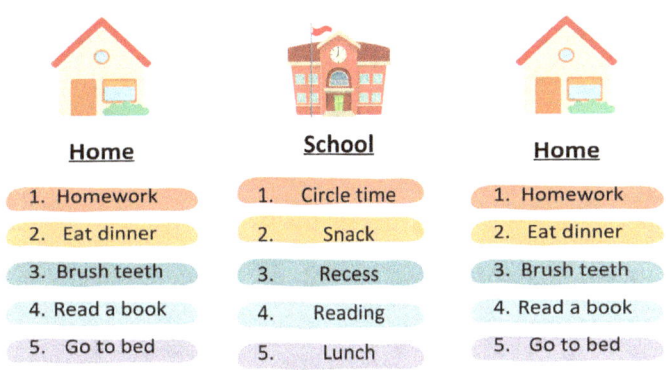

Home	School	Home
1. Homework	1. Circle time	1. Homework
2. Eat dinner	2. Snack	2. Eat dinner
3. Brush teeth	3. Recess	3. Brush teeth
4. Read a book	4. Reading	4. Read a book
5. Go to bed	5. Lunch	5. Go to bed

What am I Working For?

Why do we get out of bed in the morning? It's so warm and comfortable. If we're not being dragged out of bed by our children, why would we get up? What is the reward that can separate you from your comforter and pajamas? Money! If you don't get up and go to work, who will pay for your rent, mortgage, food, too expensive vacations, and those shoes you don't really need but really want?

Children are the same way. We shouldn't expect a child to just do everything we want them to, and get nothing in return.

We should expect them to want a reward, whether it be a physical, such as a toy, sticker, or snack, or intangible, such as verbal praise, a hug, or a high five.

What a child will work for is individual to the child. What is a highly desired reward for one,might not work for another. One child might love stickers, and another couldn't care less about getting a sticker. One child might love earning time to play with cars. One child might be thrilled to get a balloon. One child might love to get a special snack.

My son really loves going to the park to ride on the swings, having chocolate ice cream for dessert, and being able to pick out a new toy. When I need him to keep on task, get his work done, or just do his very best, I incentivize him with one of these rewards. Knowing what he's working for and what the expectations are in order to get the reward, really helps him to stay motivated. He's not perfect, no one is, so he benefits from reminders of agreement.

Token Boards

First of all, what is a token board? A token board is a visual tracker of progress towards a goal or task completion. A lot of people do well with visual input or stimuli. It goes back to the use of a multimodal system to reinforce learning. We can be verbally reminded that we have five more things to complete before we get a favored toy to play with, and this auditory stimulus is one way to keep you on track. But even with a verbal reminder, we can still get off track and distracted.

If you add a visual component, such as a token board, it will reinforce the goal, what is needed in order to achieve the goal, and how far along we are in the task completion. There are almost as many versions of a token board you can create, as there are goals to achieve. You can individualize the token board system to the child.

Find out what your child is willing to work hard for and earn. Refer back to the token board to let them know how much more they need to work in order to complete the token board and get their reward. One of my clients absolutely loved playing with popper toys. Another client loved temporary tattoos. Another client wanted me to draw him a train track on a file folder so he could put train stickers on them. Over time, I went through a lot of file folders, but it was worth it.

Examples of token boards include:

I am working for...	(Stickers)	😊
😊	😊	

First	Then
Vehicle puzzle	Bubbles

Timers

"Are we done yet?" is a question our littles ones frequently ask, especially when they're trying to get out of doing "work." We, adults, internally ask the same question several times a day, whether we realize it or not. Every time we sneak a look at our smart phone or watch to check the time, we're regulating our expectation of how long we need to continue doing a task, or how long we have until we get some kind of reward.

Not every child needs a formal attention goal, but a lot of children would benefit from paying attention to target tasks more than they do now.

Using a timer can help your child attend to a task for longer amounts of time. What happens if the timer goes off and the child is still attending and engaged in the task?

Start with a small, manageable amount of time, like three minutes. You know your kiddo best. If they can be stretched to five to ten minutes for work tasks, do that. If their attention is so poor, you lose them in less than a minute, start with one minute, and provide a ton of encouragement.

Type of timers to consider:

- Digital timer – with visual numbers like on your phone, a kitchen timer, etc.
- Analog timer – with visual indicators for time counting down.
- Sand timer – they have them for a minute, two minutes, five minutes, etc.

- Liquid motion timers – colored liquid bubbles that work similarly to sand timers.
- Light-up Countdown timer – lights up when the timer is done.

Review the Progress

When working towards a goal, I love to know how much work I've done already, and how much more I still need to do. It helps me anticipate the endurance needed to finish the task, and at the same time, cheer me about the progress made so far.

When an activity or task is completed, acknowledge the completion, and review what else is expected to be done. This not only works on memory, but it also introduces sequencing, and reinforces progress made so far.

"Great! We finished the dinosaur puzzle. We just have our picture stories and categories to complete. Then we get stickers!"

Celebrate Completion

I don't know anyone who doesn't smile when they win an award, finish a big race, or gets acknowledged at work. You don't have to win Employee of the Month to feel like a champion. It could be something small like getting acknowledged for your stellar work this week. You don't even need a physical award (although certificates and plaques do feel awesome to receive sometimes).

The same goes with our children. They work really hard. Sometimes they work really, really, really hard. Sometimes it feels like we work really, really, really hard, to get them to work. But in the end, they did it. They completed the work. They marked off all the tasks they needed to complete, and now it's time to get recognized for it.

You should celebrate completion in the exact way that makes the child grin from ear to ear, make their eyes open wide, and maybe even make them clap their hands in excitement. This "secret way" depends on the child.

Some kids love stickers, and some kids couldn't care less. Some kids love bubbles, and some couldn't care less. Some kids love balloons, and some kids couldn't care less about balloons. Some kids love swing time, and some kids are scared of the swing. Some kids love to free-play with the cars. Some kids love lollipops. The list of celebrations is endless. You just need to find out how to celebrate your kiddo. What is rewarding to them?

The Uncooperative Child

It isn't uncommon that a child doesn't want to cooperate all the time. It's actually perfectly natural and expected. My own son doesn't always want to do a work task. In fact, he almost never wants to do a work task. It takes motivation to get him, or even myself, to do work.

Paychecks are what motivates me, because it's a tangible reward. I'm not greedy, but I do need to pay my bills. I also work because I know what I do helps people. It's an intangible or an inner reward.

My son is motivated much differently. At school, he recently earned a phone call to me. He loves to call me on the phone, so the teacher utilized it as a way to get him to focus, do his work, and control any unruly behaviors. He's also motivated to earn screen time, trips to the park, and even a favorite snack.

In speech class and at home, the rewards they can earn can vary from stickers, a toy, a balloon, bubble play, to even a high five. Each child is different, and is motivated by their own individual rewards. Those rewards can change day by day too. I like to give the child a choice about what they want to work for. It makes them feel like they're in charge, and in control.

Allowing them to choose the activity they'd like to do, as well as the order in which they'd like to do them, can make them feel like you're not forcing them to do what you want them to do. They are helping to make decisions about their level of participation.

Having a timer to indicate a set amount of "work" time can help with the uncooperative child. By working for a set amount of time, such as five minutes, makes the work manageable. You can insert "break" times between the work. You may have to have more short activities, but hopefully you see the participation increase overall.

Work task	5 min
Break time	2 min
Work task	5 min
Break time	2 min
Work task	5 min
Break time	2 min

Work task	5 min
Break time	2 min
Work task	5 min
Break time	2 min
Work time	5 min
All Done (aka Reward Time)	

The Meltdown Child

We've all been exposed to the child who has gone from zero to twenty in a matter of seconds. They are now on the floor, rolling around, flailing their limbs to make chaotic dust angels, and crying their eyes out. Sometimes they really aren't crying, but they are really trying to make you, and everyone else, think they are. Some of these kiddos deserve an Oscar for their performances.

For other children, the meltdown is real, and we need to adjust how we are delivering the message for the task at hand. Another thing we must change is our response to the meltdown. It is often the natural response to match the frenetic energy of the other person, whether we realize it or not. It's important when dealing with a very upset and deregulated child, that we balance out the energy by being calm (really calm), and slowing ourselves down. It's as if we are absorbing and muting their energy in order for them to be able to be present.

Everything from our body language, to our volume of speech, our intonation, and rate of speech should communicate a sense of calm and safety. Get down to their level, rather than standing over them. Speak in a softer voice, rather than one that indicates frustration or impatience. Use a level intonation, versus a wide range of tones that may seem overwhelming. Speak slower than your normal speaking rate, so they can understand everything you say, and make them feel like the center of your attention for the moment.

If it's a formal speech therapy session, you can try having the parent sit in the session with you. The child may do better sitting on the parent's lap or at least next to the parent. If that doesn't work, you may need to end the session early, and try again the next session. You can slowly build up the time the child is able to stay in the session. Fading out the parent's proximity to the child can happen once the child is familiar and comfortable with the sessions. Eventually you can have the parent leave the room completely. Every child is different and unique. Their level of comfort will vary. You just need to be flexible and adjust.

If this child is your own, and you can't end the session early, do your very best to make your child feel safe and comforted. They may want to be cuddled. They may not want you too close. You know your child's behaviors best. You are a good parent, after all.

Let's Practice

Schedule Yourself

Even if you already use a planner, whether it be digital or old school paper, write out your daily schedule from morning until bedtime in detail. Feel free to write it out on a separate sheet if you need more space.

TIME	ACTIVITY

Schedule the Child

What does the child's schedule look like? Can you break their day down into small digestible chunks?

Home

1.

2.

3.

4.

School

1.

2.

3.

4.

? / Other

1.

2.

3.

4.

CHAPTER 7

When Should You Be "Teaching"?

The real question is, "When shouldn't you be teaching?" Approaching every situation as an opportunity to teach, will help you start to build a habit of mindfully creating a series of moments where language can be introduced, modeled, and expanded. I'm not saying it's easy to always be in a teaching mode. I like to think of it as incorporating the skills into your lifestyle, to engraine them in your interactions.

When I first started training new speech-language pathologists and speech-language pathology assistants, I really needed to think about how to break down what I did in therapy sessions into manageable parts. The way I interact with my clients happens in a very fluid way, without me really having to think about each step along the way.

Evaluating the steps needed to be done for each activity helped me understand how to see language development with a refreshed perspective. It's one of the reasons I wanted to write this book. It made me realize what I did could be taught and replicated if explained well and I provided a blueprint.

This blueprint is not set in stone. You can and should adapt it to your lifestyle, personality, and to the population you work with. The important thing is to make the strategies part of your daily habits, so that you use them whenever you come across a kiddo. You'll find you make a lot of little friends along the way.

Being as fortunate as I am to work primarily in one location, I get to spend the majority of my day seeing children, whether under my care or not. There's not one moment when I'm not using one of the many ingrained strategies when interacting with the children. It makes them feel important, confident, and excited to try out their speech and language.

Too Much, Too Soon, Is Confusing

If you've ever traveled to a foreign country where you didn't understand the language, anything said to you sounded chaotic, jumbled, and overwhelming. It's not until you are taught the new language in a very strategic and manageable way, you are able to start to understand what is being said and how you can express yourself.

I remember my first day of class in German 101. It was a ninety-minute class, and for the first half of class, our instructor only spoke in German. An immediate feeling of overwhelm came over me, and I seriously considered leaving.

I'm glad I decided to stay. Once I got over my anxiety, I realized our professor was utilizing strategies of repetition, gesturing, and facial expressions to teach us a handful of very basic questions and statements. Within forty-five minutes, our professor was able to get us to say:

- Hello
- My name is ___.

- What is your name?
- I'm from ____.
- Where are you from?

It was pretty remarkable to transition from completely not understanding anything, to being able to communicate simple sentences and questions. There was a lot of repetition of phrases and questions to help reinforce what was trying to be communicated, and how to respond appropriately.

For our kids who haven't grasped the understanding of language, the way we teach and practice language with them is so much more important. We must be mindful about how we introduce vocabulary and concepts, to build their confidence and successfulness in learning.

Start with the Target

Keep your eye on the prize. What's your target? When we're teaching, we may be overwhelmed with all the concepts, length of utterance, and articulation all at once. We need to figure out what the key element is that we're trying to teach at this present moment. The key concept could be verbs, nouns, prepositions, etc. Think of the target as the nucleus of the lesson. If we try to include every concept into every lesson, we will be spread too thin, and the learning will be diluted.

Let's start with nouns. A noun is a person, place, or thing. We can be teaching vocabulary for animals, clothing, vehicles, things around the house, rooms in a house, you name it. Familiar nouns to the child are key. What is the child exposed to in their home, at their school or daycare, and out in the community?

Once you introduce nouns, you can then move onto actions (verbs) and descriptors (adjectives).

Examples of familiar vocabulary for common categories include:

ANIMALS:
- Dog
- Cat
- Bird
- Cow
- Pig
- Sheep
- Horse

HOUSEHOLD:
- Bed
- Chair
- Table
- Door
- Couch
- Window

SCHOOL
- Desk
- Chair
- Rug
- Playground
- Paper
- Crayon
- Paint

VEHICLES
- Car
- Truck
- Boat
- Airplane
- Bus
- Motorcycle
- Tricycle

FOOD
- Water
- Milk
- Juice
- Apple
- Cracker
- Banana
- Cheese
- Cookie

DESCRIPTORS
- Big
- Little
- Colors
- Quantity
- Wet
- Dry
- Hard
- Soft
- Bumpy
- Smooth

ACTIONS
- Open
- Close
- Up
- Down
- Put in
- Put on

- Take out
- Walk
- Run
- Jump

- Drink
- Eat
- Read

Short Phrases

Now that you've identified and introduced the target word or vocabulary, let's add to it with just one or two more words. This should not be anything too long or overwhelming. By adding too much information at one time, we return to the chaos, and comprehension goes down. Without comprehension, we cannot move to expression. Here are some examples of how to extend words into short, comprehensible phrases.

Dog.
Big dog.
Big dog barks.

Apple.
Red apple.
Crunchy red apple.

Car.
Blue car.
Go, blue car.

Eat.
Eat cookie.
I eat big cookie.

Longer Sentences

Once you've expanded the target word into a short phrase, it's time to lengthen it into a longer, more specific sentence. I'm a fan of carrier phrases and sentences to help to generalize the target vocabulary into more meaningful and relatable experiences. A carrier phrase is a part of the sentence that remains the same while you are able to change one aspect of the sentence in order to practice and reinforce the vocabulary and sentence expansion. The carrier phrase can be at the beginning or the end of the sentence.

I hear the <u>big dog barking</u>.
I hear the <u>red bird tweeting</u>.
I hear the <u>orange cat meowing</u>.
I hear the <u>brown horse neighing.</u>

I eat the <u>crunchy red apple</u>.
I eat the <u>yellow banana</u>.
I eat the <u>purple grape</u>.
I eat the <u>orange orange</u>.

<u>The blue car</u> *goes fast.*
<u>The red car</u> *goes fast.*
<u>The yellow truck</u> *goes fast.*
<u>The orange motorcycle</u> *goes fast.*

Mistakes Are Okay and Expected

You may be tempted, or feel obligated, to correct every single error the child makes, in order to make sure they're learning things correctly. You may think that the mistakes they make are reflections of your teaching. It is natural to make mistakes as you're learning. It's unnatural to stop every time you make a mistake, or be expected to correct it.

Stopping to correct a mistake every time you make one is a very halting and exhausting way to function. It's very taxing on the brain to move forward, step back, move forward, step back, and so forth. There is a time for explicit teaching, and there's a time for generalization.

Explicit teaching happens in structured therapy sessions as well as in structured carry-over activities assigned outside of sessions to practice what was taught in the sessions. If a child isn't in formal speech therapy, explicit teaching can happen in the home or classroom with a parent or teacher. This is when we may break up the sentences into manageable chunks, use the strategy of tapping or clapping out syllables, or use a sing-songy delivery.

When you're generalizing what you've been teaching during highly structured lessons, you need to be more flexible with what the child is producing, and be able to model back the corrected version without making the child feel like they've made a mistake, or that you don't approve of their performance.

Language Bombardment

The term language bombardment sounds overwhelming, like you're shoving words at a child and expecting them to receive them in a rapid-fire manner. It's really not that serious. Think of language bombardment as means to introduce vocabulary and language the child is learning in a more casual and naturalistic way. The point isn't for the child to absorb then regurgitate the information exactly. It's a way for the child to get auditory stimuli supporting the areas of need the child has for language development.

I like to think about language bombardment in a visual concept of scaffolding one thing on top of another. You start with the target concept, then layer on a phrase with the target, then layer on a short sentence, then finally a longer sentence with more detail. You can continue to model more detailed sentences, varying the details while keeping the target concept central. The image of steps going up or down to a level platform may help as well.

They Don't Have to Repeat Everything

Although it's great when a child is able to accurately repeat what you said, word for word, that's not our end goal.If it were, we'd just be creating parrots. The purpose of language development is to promote natural communication between the child and their communicative partner(s).

Once they've demonstrated the ability to imitate the target sentences, and have moved onto spontaneous speech, the need to repeat everything is not necessary. We would like the child to be able to imitate the target word, phrase, or sentence, but we shouldn't expect them to continue to imitate everything we are saying. Part of the task is listening and absorbing information provided in language bombardment.

You will find a lot of children will demonstrate errors in spontaneous connected speech, especially in verb tenses. If their overall message is understood, you can repair and model back to them the corrected utterance in conversation without asking them to repeat it. It helps when you know the context which the child is speaking about.

Here are some examples for erred utterances and the repaired model:

- I eat pizza for lunch today.
- Oh. You ate pizza for lunch today?

- Doggie sheep hungry eat bubbles.
- The doggie and sheep are hungry. They want to eat bubbles.

- Mommy come back work.
- Yes, mommy will come back after work.

- I fall yesterday.
- You fell yesterday?

Let's Practice

Here are some examples of utilizing the strategies of scaffolding learned with different action words. Think of your own examples using familiar words from target vocabulary you'd like to teach your child.

CAT
1. Cat.
2. See the cat.
3. I see the cat running.
4. I see the orange cat running fast.

BABY
1. Baby.
2. Happy baby.
3. The happy baby smiles.
4. The happy baby is smiling at his mommy.

HOUSE
1. House.
2. Big House.
3. The house is big.
4. The big house is red.

BUS
1. Bus
2. Yellow bus
3. The bus is yellow.
4. The children ride the yellow bus.

APPLE
1. Apple.
2. Red apple.
3. The apple is red.
4. The red apple is crunchy.
5. I like to eat the red crunchy apple.

SHIRT
1. Shirt.
2. Blue shirt.
3. Put on a blue shirt.
4. I put on a new blue shirt.

WRITING
1. Writing
2. She is writing.
3. She is writing with a pencil.
4. She is writing in a book.

THROWING
1. Throwing.
2. He is throwing.
3. He is throwing a ball.
4. He is throwing / a white ball.

READING
1. Reading.
2. She is reading a book.
3. She is reading a book with her Daddy.
4. They are reading / a book / together.

DANCING
1. Dancing.
2. He is dancing.
3. He is dancing with his grandma.
4. They are dancing / together.

RIDING
1. Riding.
2. She is riding a bike.
3. She is wearing a helmet.
4. She is riding / a bike / with a helmet on.

Now, let's have you pick an action, noun, or adjective. Build your scaffolding off of your target vocabulary word and expand it to a phrase, a short sentence, and a longer sentence.

Action: _____

1. _____
2. _____
3. _____
4. _____

Noun: _____

1. _____
2. _____
3. _____
4. _____

Adjective: _____

1. _____

2. _____

3. _____

4. _____

CHAPTER 8

In Sight, But Just Out of Reach

Sabotage

When I use the term sabotage, I don't mean it in the traditional sense. The way I like to define *sabotage* is "creating opportunities for practice in mindful and deliberate ways." There is no destruction or damage here. There is, however, a lot of careful planning, and sometimes scheming.

I enjoy approaching a situation or scenario by brainstorming all the ways in which I can sabotage various items in order to increase opportunities to practice language. After a while of mindful practice, you'll be able to sabotage your child's life with ease, in the most helpful ways possible, of course.

Snack time and mealtime are great for creating opportunities to practice requesting, especially if the child has a good appetite and favorite food items. Goldfish crackers are a perfect example of how to utilize sabotage. Who doesn't love Goldfish crackers? As caregivers, we've all filled a bowl with Goldfish, or another favorite snack, and just put it in front of the child to enjoy. When we do that, we take away opportunities for the child to practice language.

Instead of giving all of the snacks, you can give the child one or two pieces. Have the remainder of the snack nearby, in sight, but out of reach. I like to give the container a little shake to tempt the child. You can even bring the container near the child and then quickly move it out of reach. The purpose of this is to get the child to communicate interest and desire for more snacks. They might reach out for the snack, point to their empty bowl, or even whine or cry. This is all a part of communication.

Here are some other areas of your daily life you can find opportunities to sabotage your child:

- Put your child's favorite toy on a high shelf.
- Give them an empty cup.
- Hide their pillow at bedtime.
- Hide some puzzle pieces from a puzzle they're working on.
- Give them only two French fries.
- Give them only one sock.
- Give them bubbles without a wand.
- Put a favored small toy in a very hard to open container.

Repetition Is Key

The key to mastering anything is practice. Professional athletes log in hundreds of thousands of practice hours to be the best at their game. In order for a child to learn to walk, they must first spend countless hours practicing the steps and sequences, even just to get up and balanced. They will have numerous falls and wobbles along the way to begin toddling.

The same goes for understanding and expressing language. For those of us who've tried learning a second language, we know the struggles of first comprehending the foreign tongue, before we can even begin to attempt to speak it. The more we listen to new words and phrases, the easier it gets to decipher the differences in sounds, and to break those sounds into individual words.

The more opportunities we give our children to practice their language, the better they will get at using language more independently and naturally. The repetition builds connections in the brain that will be lifelong, like riding a bike. Once you get it down, you really don't have to think about it.

What Would They "Die" For?

Depending on the day and my mood, I'd die to have a dozen oysters, for some Hawaiian shaved ice, or maybe a really amazing massage after a long day. Whatever it may be, we all have something we would "die" for. It could be a food, a place, a thing, or just a moment in peace, snuggled up with a fuzzy blanket in silence. For every individual person out there, their "die for" is as individual as they are.

It's our job to find out what our kids would "die" for, or at least work really hard for. Some children really love things to eat. They might work for Goldfish, or some blueberries. Some children really like music. They might like to play with a rain stick or bells. Some kids love vehicles or animals. They might like to play with a school bus or dinosaur. Whatever you decide to use as your temptation, make sure they not only like it, but that they love it (aka "would die for it).

Here are some examples to try out:

- Bubbles
- Vehicles
- Puzzles
- Food
- Drinks
- Balls
- Musical instruments
- Dolls/figurines
- Cause and effect toys
- Light machine
- Blocks
- Radio or music player
- Books
- Play food

Up High, Down Low, Just Out of Reach

When you're a little kiddo who's just over two feet tall, anything higher than a tabletop is really high. When you're a kiddo in a highchair, anything that might be on the floor is really low. The impossible task of reaching the desired items helps to create opportunities to utilize language, whether it be a grunt, gesture, picture card exchange, pointing board, simple sign, close approximation of sounds, or even the actual words we understand.

Once you have found out what your child's favorite thing is, you can place it on the bookshelf just out of reach. The item will be visible, but they can't quite get to it. You want to make sure the child isn't going to try and climb the bookshelf, of course. The objective is to tempt the child into wanting the item, and hopefully have them utilize communication in order to get the item.

The overall goal for them is that they will talk. But, until they are able to verbally communicate what they want, we'll be happy with any number of indications of wanting the desired item. The child may look at the item, point to it, reach for it, or grunt, yell, or babble.

Our response to the varied level of communication should be to model what you think they are trying to communicate. I like to speak as if I were speaking for them, then add on your own natural reply.

Child: (points toward ball)
You: "Ball, I want ball."
Give them the ball and say, "Here you go. Have the ball."

Child: (looking at sippy cup)
You: "Yummy juice, I want juice."
Give them the juice and say, "Here you go. Have some juice."

Child: Babbles unintelligibly while looking at a toy car.
You: "Look at the car. I want car. Vroom vroom."
Give them the car and say, "Here you go. You can have the car."

As the child's babbling starts to evolve into real words, you can require them to make more of an effort before giving the item up. They have demonstrated communicative intent, as well as vocalizations. You can push their skills a bit to have them say the initial sound of the target word, produce a close approximation of the target word, or demonstrate a simple sign for "more" or "please."

Let's Practice

Think about three things your child would "die" for, or at least work really hard for.

1. _____

2. _____

3. _____

Now, think about how you could manipulate each of these things in order for your child to indicate they want the item(s).

1. _____

2. _____

3. _____

CHAPTER 9

Which One?

What Do They Want?

We've all been in that situation where you can't figure out what the child wants. I've certainly been there before, and I'm not going back. They definitely want something in the general area of the kitchen. So you start holding up things and asking, "Do you want this?" It's not what they wanted. You hold up something else, and again ask, "Do you want this?" Still not the right thing. After holding up five different things, one after the other, and asking the same question, you're left frustrated, exhausted, and stumped.

Maybe you just give up and give the child what you want them to have. If the child has an idea of what they want, and what you give them is not what they want, you may be in for some crying, tantrums, and headaches. No one wants that.

It'd be great if we were mind readers, but we're not. We may not have superpowers, but we can learn some super-strategies to help make our interactions with our little ones go smoother. These strategies are simple changes to how we can accommodate our young learners. Although they are simple, they may not feel completely natural at first. It's important to practice them mindfully and deliberately until they become a habit. Before you know it, they'll become second nature.

By following some simple strategies, you can help to figure out what the child wants.

- Model the vocabulary.
- Hold the items at least shoulder width apart.
- Pay attention to eye gaze.
- Provide the language you'd expect them to use if they were able to speak well.
- Give the wrong one (if you want to test if they're really paying attention).

Model the Vocabulary

We can't expect a child to name what they want if they don't know the name of what they want. Remember, language is learned, not innate. We aren't born knowing the names of things, actions, feelings, etc. Some children are able to pick up vocabulary effortlessly. Some children struggle. Let's make it easy by modeling the vocabulary we want them to learn.

When my son was little, I would ask him, "Which shirt do you want to wear? The green one or the blue one?" At the same time, I would be holding up the two shirts, shoulder width apart, extending the colored shirt I was referring to match what I was saying.

You can do this with just about anything. For example, when playing with race cars, you can hold two different color cars and ask, "Do you want the red car or the black car?" You can also model different sizes, such as, "Do you want the big truck or the little truck?"

Hearing the vocabulary and seeing what item each of the words matches with it, will help to build comprehension. It utilizes the multimodal systems of vision and hearing, which I often find helpful in solidifying information learning.

Shoulder Width Apart

Okay, great! You're holding up two things the child might want. You're also providing the vocabulary to accompany the items, "Do you want the apple or banana?" The only thing wrong is that you're holding the items right next to each other, and your child can't speak just yet. They may reach out for both items, and you're back to not knowing exactly what they wanted.

This is an easy fix. Hold the items at least shoulder width apart. You will easily be able to see what item the child wants by observing their eyes scanning to the item, or by the turning of their head towards the item.

Sometimes the child is really quick, and still tries to grab both items at the same time. When this happens, pay close attention to which item they glanced at first. Immediately hold that item out to the child to indicate that's the item they've chosen.

Another option is to show the child each item directly in front of you, while asking them if they would like that item. Then remove that item from their visual field while presenting the next item. After this, remove both items from their visual field, then bring them back, but now shoulder width apart, rather than right in front of them.

Eye Gaze is an Okay Start

You're presenting your two options correctly, shoulder width apart. You're providing the appropriate vocabulary. You wait, and the child says nothing. Don't worry—you didn't do anything wrong, and neither did the child.

The child will likely give you some indication of their choice, even if it's a fleeting eye gaze to the desired item. It's important you tune in and pay close attention to what the child does during the presentation of the items, and directly after you make the offering. The eye gaze may be only momentary, so you really need to be decisive with your follow up.

Once you've been given the indication of their choice, communicate with them as if they are using words to make their choice,, and respond to them with a model of what they requested.

"I want the green shirt."
"Good choice. Here you go. Here's the green shirt."

Give the Wrong One

I enjoy finding ways to sabotage a child, especially when they are emerging with functional language. If you always gave the child the correct item, in therapy or life, it would probably go pretty smoothly, yes. They ask for something, you give it to them. They ask for something else, you give it to them, and so forth. Where's the fun in that?

In order to make sure a child is paying attention, I'll purposefully give them the wrong item. This is not because I necessarily want to "mess with them," but I'm seeing if they are paying attention, how they will react to being given the wrong thing, and if they have the language and vocabulary to protest.

If the child is at a very low level of language acquisition and understanding, they will likely just take the wrong item you are handing them, and be totally okay with it. For this child, this technique of giving the wrong one is too advanced, and should be revisited later, once their receptive and expressive language has progressed.

For the child with adequate receptive language or comprehension skills, this strategy of giving the wrong item is perfect for them. This child understands what they want. Even if they can't fully express themselves, they know what they desire, and can comprehend what is given to them.

Let's Practice

Fill in the blanks for choices from each category below.

FOOD

Do you want to eat _____ or do you want to eat _____?

DRINKS

Do you want to drink _____ or do you want to drink_____?

VEHICLES

Do you want _____ or do you want _____?

COLORS

Do you want the _____ ball or do you want the _____ ball?

BOOKS

Do you want to read _____ or do you want to read _____?

CLOTHES

Do you want to wear _____ or do you want to wear _____?

CHAPTER 10

Sequencing

It's never too early to introduce sequencing. Even though the child isn't able to understand and express what is first, next, and last, you can still get them used to the cadence of something happening, and then something else happens.

I would plan three to five things for our day, and sequence them with my son, Che. I would say to him, "First, we're having breakfast, then we'll change clothes, then we'll brush our teeth, and then we'll go to school." When we completed one of the tasks, I'd review our list, saying "We finished breakfast, now let's change clothes and brush our teeth before we go to school."

Now, Che will spontaneously sequence out what he needs to do to get ready for school, or will let me know the things we will be doing for the day, in order. Sometimes I ask him to remind me to do something after we finish _____. It helps him stay present in the moment, work on his short-term memory, and helps me with my mommy brain.

It may be helpful to utilize the "FIRST/THEN" board introduced in Chapter Six to assist in reinforcing the auditory direction of doing the activities with a visual component. By having the information provided through a multimodal system, you are able to tap into different learning styles. Some people are auditory learners. Some people are visual learners. Putting together the learning styles can only help, not hinder, learning.

Strategies for Sequencing

They say that change is the spice of life. Sometimes you might want to switch up the order to keep things fresh. By doing so, you're also having them listen to different instructions and choices, which mirrors the variety we experience in daily life. Having things happen in the same way all the time makes it monotonous and predictable.

At times, the child may not want to tell you which activity they want to do first. It may be because they don't want to work, they're shy, they don't understand the request, or they don't like being told what to do, (aka, you're "being bossy").

When we have two activities to complete, I will tell the child, "We are going to do _____ and ____. Which one should we do last?" It implies that we are going to do one or the other activity first, which in turn implies we will be doing the activities no matter what. It's a sneaky way to make the child feel in charge, and get them to somewhat agree to do the work.

First, Next, Last

As you are able to practice simple sequencing several times, maybe a hundred times, you can start expecting them to grasp three-step sequences.

I love using self-correcting, picture sequencing puzzles to practice the concepts of "first, next, last." The pictures provide a visual component to go along with your verbal descriptions of them. The self-correcting aspect of the puzzle allows the child to work on problem solving, visual spatial awareness, and independence.

If you don't have self-correcting picture sequencing puzzles, you can utilize pictures, either pre-made or drawn out. You can even take pictures of real-life sequences and print them out. Be creative and don't worry about your materials being "perfect."

When your child is able to consistently sequence 3-picture sequences correctly, you can increase the difficulty of the task by increasing the steps of the sequence to four and five-steps. Ideally, the child will be able to imitate the sentences that go along with each picture, then progress to spontaneously producing their own sentences to describe each step.

First, the car is dirty.	Next, she is washing the car.	Last, the car is all clean.

Other Ways to Incorporate Sequencing

I like to utilize containers, such as baskets or trays, during my speech therapy sessions, to act as the steps of the sequence we will be completing for the session. The visual containers help to reinforce the auditory information I'm providing. When one activity is done, we can empty the container and put the activity that was in the container into an "All Done" container.

As we complete the activities, I will review what we completed, and what else we need to get done. By seeing the empty containers, the child has a sense of accomplishment, and knows what the expectation of the session is.

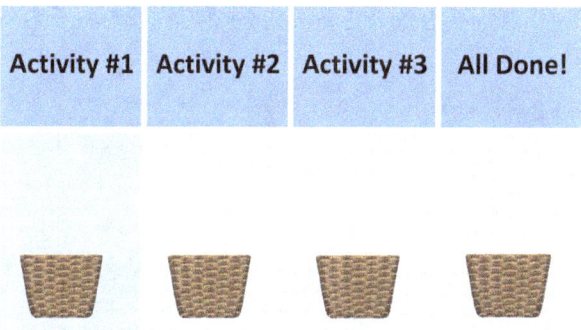

You can also start sequencing activities of daily life, such as dressing in the morning, making a peanut butter and jelly sandwich, or what steps we do when we get in a car. Breaking down the activity into small, three-step chunks, will allow moving onto longer sequences to be a more natural progression. Soon enough, you'll be following a recipe and making a delicious meal. Maybe not just yet though. Some examples are as follows.

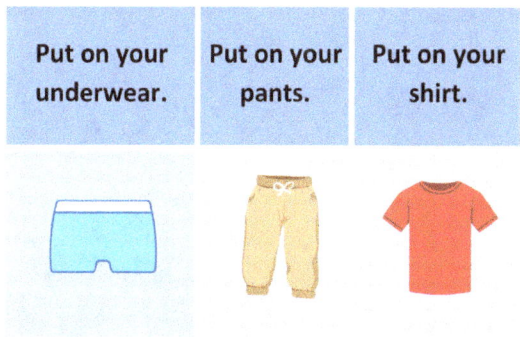

Put peanut butter on one slice of bread.	Put Jelly on another slice of bread.	Put the two pieces of bread together.

Get in your seat.	Buckle your seatbelt.	Ready to go!

Let's Practice

Practice writing out simple three-step sequences that are familiar to you and your child's day.

First,	Next,	Last,

First,	Next,	Last,

First,	Next,	Last,

CHAPTER 11

Keep the Conversation Going

I'll admit, even after twenty-two years of being a practicing speech-language pathologist, sometimes I have no idea what a child is saying. We're not given magical ears along with our graduate degrees that translate gibberish into fluent words. I wish it were the case, but that's just impossible.

Before a child learns to say words, they babble. They start with babbling single sounds, usually a consonant plus a vowel, such as "dadada," or "mamama," which is why a lot of first words sound like the child said, "Dada," or, "Mama." Eventually, children start mixing different consonants and vowel combinations. They mimic the inflection they hear from people who interact with them. Before you know it, the child is sounding like they are trying to speak to you, but in some foreign language that we like to fondly refer to as "gibberish."

Fill in the Blanks

I love meeting little kiddos who are curious, active, and downright unintelligible. A child may ramble on with a string of babbling sounds, loaded with rising and falling intonations, indicating a slew of information for their very important message. They look at you, expecting you to understand and respond back with praise or excitement. You might think that all you can do is smile politely, but really, there is so much you can do to help fill in the blanks.

When a child is speaking, especially when they are unintelligible, you need to observe their surroundings, their facial expressions, their gestures, and listen to their intonation to help decipher what it is they are trying to say. You need to play the detective, and investigate all the clues to make an educated guess about the topic. If they are commenting or asking a question, you should observe what emotions are involved in their communication, and so on and so forth.

Ask Questions

In any normal situation in which we do not understand what a colleague or friend is saying, we simply ask questions. You naturally want clarification on what's confusing. It should be the same when you're interacting with children. The interaction between two individuals is dependent upon communication, how things are expressed, and how things are understood.

Asking simple questions is great in aiding clarification. This is when asking a yes or no question is completely acceptable. You can also ask questions about different guesses you have about the topic, based on the intonation and sounds of the babbling.

Are you talking about the beach?

Did you see a bear or a bird?

What did you eat? A cake or a steak?

Did you have fun?

Was it cold or hot?

Did Mommy take you to the party?

Did you have money or a monkey?

Make Comments

It's rare that a child is still. They're always doing something. Even when they haven't started talking yet, they may be rolling around, dropping things, putting things in their mouths, or sometimes they just stare out a window. If they aren't doing the talking, then you should be.

The key elements to conversation are a series of comments (or statements) and questions. I like to picture a conversation as a train with many cars attached to it. The conversation starts with the engine, then the tender is added, along with the passenger car, the dining car, and so on and so forth. Each section of the train represents a question or a statement. A person may link more than one car to the train at a time, such as when answering a question, one might follow up with another question, or make an additional comment.

When you are interacting with a child or person who is unable to participate in linking up train cars on their own, you must step in to build the train yourself, while continuing to engage your communicative partner in the experience. It sounds like a lot of work, and it is at first. You'll be making all the comments and asking all the questions. It may sound confusing, but think of it as reading both parts of a dialogue from a play or movie. The more you practice having a conversation (with yourself), the easier it gets.

I like your shirt.

What color is your shirt?

Your shirt is green.

What color is my shirt?

My shirt Is blue.

We both have shirts.

What color shirt does Michael have?

His shirt is red.

Be Animated

We have all experienced that learning and remembering things is easier when they are presented in a dynamic way. I am sure you have had experiences with boring teachers or even more boring lessons that demonstrate this idea. I certainly have. I can tell you I used to forget a lot when I was in those classes. I can also tell you that I learned and retained a lot more when more of my senses were stimulated.

When someone is animated, their movements are bigger. They may be standing or crouching. Their arms may be waving over their head like they've won first place, or pulled in tight to show they're afraid. Their facial expressions are bigger, and their eyes may be round circles in surprise, or scrunched up to see in the darkness. Their voice has variations in pitch, expanding in range from very high to very low. The volume of their speech may go from a whisper like a mouse, to a loud booming trumpet, and then back down again to the level of a soft, purring kitty.

If you love eating chocolate chip cookies, you REALLY LOVE EATING CHOCOLATE CHIP COOKIES!!! If you are afraid of a noise in the dark, you're REALLY AFRAID OF THE NOISE IN THE DARK!! If you need to be quiet because your little sister is asleep, you whisper barely audible to your friend "*Shhhh. . . we need to be really, really quiet.*"

I recently told a client's mom to review some of the child's favorite songs, but with a slower rate to help with elongating the words to increase clarity. I asked her to channel her best musical theater self and be overdramatic, using big gestures, facial expressions, and body movements. This mom was up for the challenge and was excited to give this strategy a try.

Working on language with a high interest activity, such as a child's favorite song, is a great way to motivate your child to participate and have fun at the same time. They won't even realize they're "working."

Keep it Going

Most of us have been on the end of an awkward conversation where there's silence, you don't know if you should be talking, and you wonder why the other person isn't talking. A conversation with a kiddo shouldn't be that way. If there is silence, help them out by filling it in.

Think about what other comments you could make, or what questions you could ask. You're the expert in how conversations work anyways. You've been talking for way more years than they have. By helping them fill in the conversation, you are modeling language, making them feel included, and setting them up for when they're ready to jump back in.

If they make a mistake in verb tense, pronouns, or just don't make any sense, it's okay! Model the correction, but don't make them imitate it. Investigate the unknown, and find out some clues to what they meant to say. It's okay for you to guess about what they are trying to say. Your engagement and investment give meaning to the interaction, and encourages the child to continue the conversation.

A conversation is a series of comments and questions on a common topic. The topic may branch into various topics, hopefully related to each other in some kind of way, but sometimes we think in tangents, and so can our little counterparts. Once children become more practiced with conversation, we'd expect them to stay on topic more often than not. Until then, it's okay to jump from talking about breakfast, to playing in the mud, to the buzzing bee passing by.

Try to think again about the conversation starting out as a single train engine. We slowly add one more car to the train.

Eventually the train gets longer and longer as it moves along the track. Soon, the train will come to a fork in the track. The train may continue straight, veer to the left, or veer to the right. Whichever direction the train ends up going, it remains whole, connected, and moving forward.

Remember, we are always teaching, growing skills, and practicing strategies with our children. Once you grasp the concepts and apply them often enough, you won't be able to stop yourself from utilizing these skills with your own children, as well as with any other children you are fortunate to interact with.

Let's Practice

Set a timer for five minutes and engage in a "conversation" with your child, or a child you find to be unintelligible. If you make it to five minutes without it being excruciatingly painful, increase the time to ten, fifteen, then twenty minutes.

Keep in mind the strategies we just learned:

- Fill in the blanks.
- Ask questions.
- Make comments.
- Be animated.
- Keep it going.

How'd it go? Evaluate your interaction and how you felt the child responded to the strategies you applied.

_____

_____

_____

_____

_____

_____

_____

_____

_____